SPOTLIGHT ON EARTH SCIENCE

# VOLCANOES

SHAYE REYNOLDS

**PowerKiDS**
press™

NEW YORK

Published in 2017 by The Rosen Publishing Group, Inc.
29 East 21st Street, New York, NY 10010

Editor: Caitie McAneney
Book design: Michael Flynn
Interior layout: Reann Nye

Photo Credits: Cover Fotos593/Shutterstock.com; p. 4 Ammit Jack/Shutterstock.com; p. 5 Alexander Piragis/Shutterstock.com; p. 6 Burben/Shutterstock.com; p. 7 fluidworkshop/Shutterstock.com; p. 8 Ralph White/Corbis Documentary/Getty Images; p. 9 by wildestanimal/Moment Open/Getty Images; p. 10 bierchen/Shutterstock.com; p. 11 https://commons.wikimedia.org/wiki/File:MSH80_eruption_mount_st_helens_05-18-80-dramatic-edit.jpg; p. 12 yggdrasill/Shutterstock.com; p. 13 (Sunset Crater) Tim Roberts Photography/Shutterstock.com; p. 13 (Mount Fuji) Vitoony Yawilerng/Shutterstock.com; p. 14 Planet Observer/Universal Images Group/Getty Images; p. 15 https://commons.wikimedia.org/wiki/File:Tamu_Massif,_the_Earth%27s_largest_volcano,_about_1,000_Miles_east_of_Japan.jpg; p. 16 https://commons.wikimedia.org/wiki/File:Vesuvius_from_Pompeii_(hires_version_2_scaled).png; p. 17 Angelo DeSantis/Moment/Getty Images; p. 18 Roger Ressmeyer/Corbis/VCG/Corbis Documentary/Getty Images; p. 19 https://commons.wikimedia.org/wiki/File:Dave_Johnston_with_gas-detection_instrument_at_Mount_St._Helens,_4_April_1980_(USGS)_1.jpg; p. 20 Science & Society Picture Library/SSPL/Getty Images; p. 21 Gerhard Joren/LightRocket/Getty Images; p. 22 SnorriThor/Shutterstock.com.

Cataloging-in-Publication Data

Names: Reynolds, Shaye.
Title: Volcanoes / Shaye Reynolds.
Description: New York : PowerKids Press, 2017. | Series: Spotlight on earth science | Includes index.
Identifiers: ISBN 9781499425420 (pbk.) | ISBN 9781499425451 (library bound) | ISBN 9781499425437 (6 pack)
Subjects: LCSH: Volcanoes--Juvenile literature.
Classification: LCC QE521.3 R49 2017 | DDC 551.21--dc23

Manufactured in China

CPSIA Compliance Information: Batch #BW17PK For further information contact Rosen Publishing, New York, New York at 1-800-237-9932.

# CONTENTS

# CHAPTER ONE

# WHAT ARE VOLCANOES?

What's hiding underneath the surface of the earth? What materials make up the ground beneath our feet? Volcanoes give us a glimpse into the earth. They are rock formations that act as vents. These vents are openings in the earth's surface that allow gases, **debris**, and liquid rock to come out.

People usually imagine lava when they think of volcanic eruptions. However, some volcanoes just let out hot ash and debris.

Not all volcanoes are dangerous, or unsafe. In fact, many haven't erupted in a very long time. However, some volcanoes are active. That means they're erupting or expected to erupt soon. Some eruptions are major explosions. Ash and lava burst into the air, and sometimes lava flows down the side of the volcano. Luckily, volcanologists, or scientists who study volcanoes, **monitor** active volcanoes to learn when they might erupt again. Let's learn more about these amazing, explosive landforms!

# CHAPTER TWO

# A VOLCANO IS FORMED

To find out how a volcano forms, you have to know about the different layers of our planet. Earth isn't just one big ball. There are four layers, and they get hotter as you get nearer to Earth's center.

The crust is the part of Earth that you're most familiar with. It's the ground you walk on every day. Underneath the

This volcano in Iceland is just letting off steam!

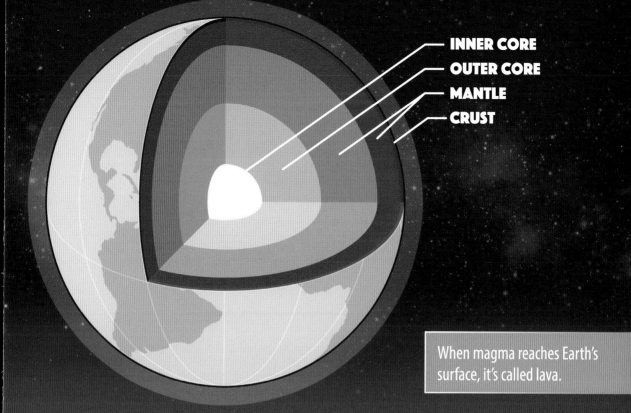

INNER CORE
OUTER CORE
MANTLE
CRUST

When magma reaches Earth's surface, it's called lava.

crust is a layer called the mantle. The mantle is partly solid and partly made of rock so hot it can flow. That liquid rock is called magma. The upper mantle and the crust together are called the lithosphere. Underneath the mantle are the outer core and the inner core. The pressure and heat in these layers are even greater than in the mantle.

Sometimes magma wells up underneath the crust, and heat and debris escape through an opening. That's a volcano!

# CHAPTER THREE

# VOLCANOES UNDERWATER

You might imagine that volcanoes are always aboveground mountains with openings on top. However, most eruptions on Earth take place underwater. In fact, scientists believe that more than 75 percent of eruptions happen deep in the sea. These underwater eruptions shape the seafloor.

Scientists have discovered **habitats** full of odd ocean creatures around underwater volcanoes.

Earth's lithosphere is broken into puzzle pieces called tectonic plates. They rest on top of the mantle's magma. Underwater volcanic activity often happens at places where tectonic plates come apart. As they part, magma rushes up to the seafloor.

What happens when hot lava meets the cold ocean water? It hardens quickly into rounded bunches of basalt rock called "pillow lava." This creates part of a new layer of crust and can build up into underwater mountains, called seamounts. The Hawaiian Islands were formed by underwater volcanoes that grew above the water's surface.

# CHAPTER FOUR

# ERUPTION!

Two major kinds of volcanic eruptions are effusive eruptions and explosive eruptions. In effusive eruptions, magma rises through the opening and flows out of the volcano as lava. In explosive eruptions, lava breaks into pieces called pyroclasts and explodes through the opening.

There are also several different eruption styles. Some volcanoes emit, or let out, gas only. Some volcanoes let out clouds of **pumice** and ash high into the sky. They may also let out lava. These eruptions, called Plinian eruptions, can last for days.

The 1980 eruption of Mount Saint Helens in Washington State was a Plinian eruption.

In some volcanoes, magma wells up to the earth's surface and escapes through vents as jets of lava. These "fire fountains" can last for hours or days! These are called Hawaiian eruptions. When lava explosions happen at regular or irregular **intervals**, they're called Strombolian eruptions. These eruptions happen when large bubbles of gas burst inside the volcano.

# CHAPTER FIVE

# TYPES OF VOLCANOES

There are a few different types of volcanoes on Earth. The easiest type to recognize is a cinder cone volcano. Most have a crater, or bowl-shaped hole, at the top. Cinder cones have a single vent from which lava explodes into the air.

Shield volcanoes have gentle slopes and a dome-like shape which resembles a soldier's shield. They're often very large and wide volcanoes. They usually have a central vent or a bunch of vents from which lava flows in all directions. When lava hardens, it adds to the volcano's slope.

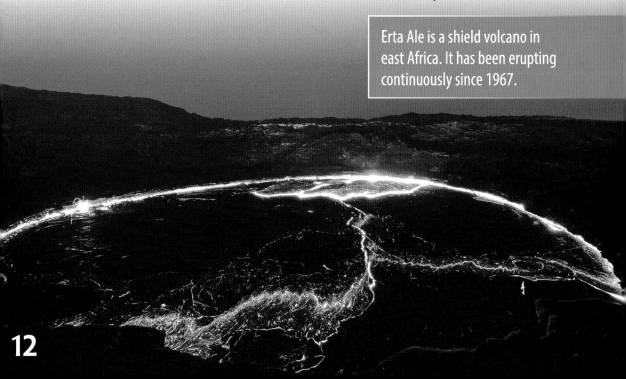

Erta Ale is a shield volcano in east Africa. It has been erupting continuously since 1967.

MOUNT FUJI, JAPAN
STRATOVOLCANO

SUNSET CRATER, ARIZONA
CINDER CONE VOLCANO

Stratovolcanoes, which are also called composite volcanoes, are very tall with steep slopes. They often have a central vent or group of vents on top. Lava flows through breaks and cracks in the volcano and hardens, which greatly strengthens the volcano over time.

# CHAPTER SIX

# WORLD'S LARGEST VOLCANOES

The tallest volcano on Earth is Mauna Kea, which is located in Hawaii. Mauna Kea is also the tallest mountain in the world. Part of it is aboveground, but most of it is underwater. From base to peak, Mauna Kea is more than

Mauna Kea is considered a **dormant** volcano because it hasn't erupted for about 4,500 years.

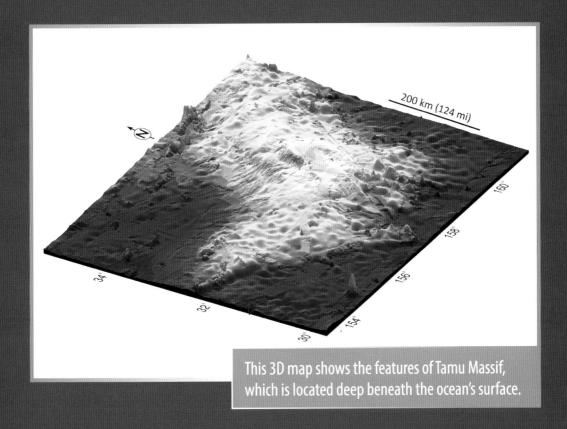

200 km (124 mi)

This 3D map shows the features of Tamu Massif, which is located deep beneath the ocean's surface.

33,500 feet (10,210.8 m) tall. Other huge volcanoes in Hawaii include Kilauea and Mauna Loa, which are found on the Big Island of Hawaii in Hawaii Volcanoes National Park.

The largest of all known volcanoes on Earth is called Tamu Massif. It's located underwater, deep in the northwestern Pacific Ocean. It covers about 120,000 square miles (310,798.6 sq km), which is nearly the size of the state of New Mexico! Despite its huge size, Tamu Massif wasn't discovered until 2013. Its gentle slopes and **isolated** location kept it a secret from scientists until just recently.

# CHAPTER SEVEN

# MOST ACTIVE VOLCANOES ON EARTH

Earth is home to many dormant volcanoes. Some volcanoes erupt often and are considered active. One of the most active volcanoes on Earth is Kilauea in Hawaii. Kilauea erupts regularly, and it sometimes erupts with slow-flowing lava for years at a time. There is a lake of lava located near the **summit** of the volcano. The nearby volcano of Mauna Loa has been active for more than 700,000 years, and it usually lets out slow lava flows.

Stromboli volcano in southern Italy has erupted regularly for more than 2,000 years. It glows red with each gas explosion, and some people call it the "Lighthouse of the Mediterranean." Mount Vesuvius, which is also in Italy, is one of the most famous volcanoes. In AD 79, this volcano destroyed the city of Pompeii. It erupts about every 20 years, but it hasn't erupted since 1944. It's long overdue!

These are the ruins of Pompeii with Mount Vesuvius in the background.

Indonesia's most active volcano is Merapi, which means "mountain of fire." In 2010, an eruption killed more than 350 people.

# CHAPTER EIGHT

# VOLCANO TECHNOLOGY

Predicting when a volcano may erupt can save many lives. Volcanologists monitor volcanoes by testing for earthquakes, volcanic gas, and ground movement. They also test the water and rocks around a volcano to learn more about the conditions there.

Ultraviolet spectrometers are tools that help scientists tell the amount of a certain volcanic gas, sulfur dioxide, that's

In the past, volcanologists had to go directly to a volcano to track changes and test the surroundings. It was very dangerous. David A. Johnston, a well-known volcanologist, was killed while monitoring Mount Saint Helens during its eruption in 1980.

DAVID A. JOHNSTON

in a cloud. **GPS** sensors may be set up around volcanoes to track movement in the ground. Drones, or unmanned aircraft, can fly over a volcano. They can hold cameras, sensors, and sampling bottles.

Volcanologists can use thermal infrared technology to predict eruptions. Thermal infrared technology captures images of the energy that is **radiated** from a landform. Heat is an **indicator** of an eruption. This technology helps volcanologists track the patterns of heat within a volcano. **Satellites** in space often take these thermal infrared images.

# CHAPTER NINE

# BENEFITS OF VOLCANOES

It's estimated that about 10 percent of Earth's human population lives near a volcano. Volcanoes have the ability to harm many people. However, volcanoes also benefit people and animals in many ways.

The soil around volcanoes is very rich. When a volcano emits ash, the ash showers down on the ground and creates healthy soil for farming. In 2011, scientists discovered that some ancient Maya cities were built on land that had been showered in volcanic ash. Scientists believe

GREAT GEYSIR, ICELAND

These people are taking a relaxing sand bath in mineral-rich sand near a volcano in Japan. The sand is heated by a hot spring.

that air currents often carried ash from nearby volcanoes to the huge ancient Maya city of Tikal.

The area on and around volcanoes is also often rich in metals, such as gold and silver. There may be many gems, such as peridots and diamonds. Volcanic activity often causes hot springs, or pools of naturally heated water. Sometimes people sit in these hot springs for health and relaxation.

# CHAPTER TEN

# LET'S VISIT VOLCANOES!

Volcanoes are some of the most amazing landforms on Earth. Many people travel from around the world to visit huge volcanoes, both active and dormant. Where can you visit a volcano?

Unless you have an underwater vehicle, you won't see the many underwater volcanoes in the ocean. However, you can visit Mauna Loa and Kilauea in Hawaii Volcanoes National Park. Many people visit volcanoes in Iceland. There are about 130 volcanoes in this small country, and many of them are active. That's because Iceland is part of a mostly underwater system of mountains called the Mid-Atlantic Ridge.

Volcanoes can teach us a lot about plate tectonics and the layers of the earth. They are a direct result of plate movement and the meeting of magma and lithosphere. Volcanoes continue to shape the earth with each awesome eruption!

# GLOSSARY

**debris** (deh-BREE) The remains of something that has broken apart.

**dormant** (DOHR-muhnt) In an inactive state.

**GPS** (JEE-PEE-ESS) A navigating system that uses satellite signals to tell the user where they are and direct them to a destination.

**habitat** (HAA-buh-tat) The natural place where an animal or plant lives.

**indicator** (IN-duh-kay-tuhr) A sign that shows the existence or condition of something.

**interval** (IHN-tuhr-vuhl) A period of time between events.

**isolated** (EYE-suh-lay-tuhd) Separate from others.

**monitor** (MAH-nuh-tuhr) To watch carefully.

**pumice** (PUH-muhs) A volcanic rock that's gray in color, lightweight, and full of small holes.

**radiate** (RAY-dee-ayt) To send out energy in rays.

**satellite** (SAA-tuh-lyt) An object that circles Earth to collect and send information or aid in communication.

**summit** (SUH-miht) The top of a mountain.

# INDEX

# PRIMARY SOURCE LIST

**Page 11**
Mount Saint Helens eruption. Photograph. Taken by Austin Post, United States Geological Survey. May 18, 1980. Skamania County, Washington State.

**Page 19**
Geologist Dave Johnston using a correlation spectrometer. Photograph. April 4, 1980. Mount Saint Helens, Skamania County, Washington.

**Page 20**
The Great Geysir. Lithograph. Created by J. Baynes, based on a drawing by Sir John Thomas Stanley Bart. Printed by Charles Joseph Hullmandel. 1789.

# WEBSITES

Due to the changing nature of Internet links, PowerKids Press has developed an online list of websites related to the subject of this book. This site is updated regularly. Please use this link to access the list: www.powerkidslinks.com/soes/volc